Doggie
PADDLIN'

David and Linda Mullally

FALCON®

Guilford, Connecticut

*To all the wonderful four-legged furry friends,
who enrich our lives as companions
on land and water*

FALCON®

An imprint of Globe Pequot

Falcon and FalconGuides are registered trademarks of Rowman & Littlefield.

Distributed by NATIONAL BOOK NETWORK

Copyright © 2017 by Rowman & Littlefield

All photos by David Mullally unless noted otherwise.

British Library Cataloguing-in-Publication Information available

Library of Congress Cataloging-in-Publication Data available

ISBN 978-1-4930-2724-8 (paperback)

ISBN 978-1-4930-2725-5 (e-book)

∞™ The paper used in this publication meets the minimum requirements of American National Standard for Information Sciences—Permanence of Paper for Printed Library Materials, ANSI/NISO Z39.48-1992.

Printed in the United States of America

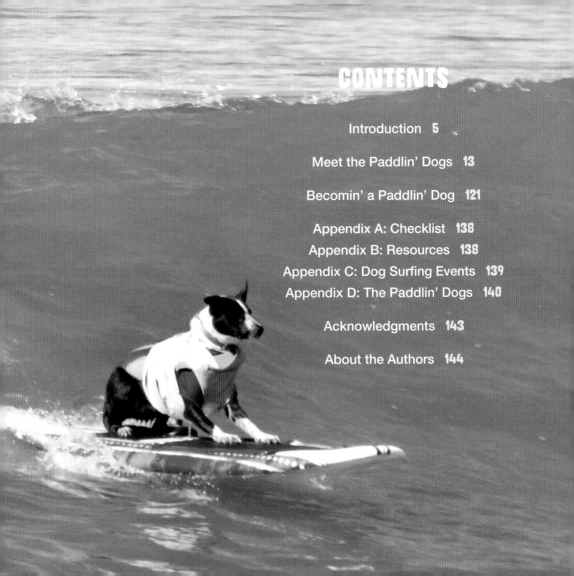

CONTENTS

IS THIS THE POSE GEORGE WASHINGTON
HAD CROSSING THE DELAWARE?

INTRODUCTION

*L*inda and I have been writing about and photographing dogs for more than twenty-five years, but when the idea for *Doggie Paddlin'* was presented to us, we knew we were in for a special challenge. I embraced it immediately, but Linda had some trepidation, and rightly so. It's one thing to photograph dogs as they wag their way toward you on the trail. The camera is always in hand, ready to capture candid shots at a moment's notice, with feet and paws all on land. Add water to the mix, and I had to be ready for wet, windy, and wavy. This called for a new mind-set, gear, and wardrobe, starting with a waterproof camera and water-compatible footwear at the top of the list. Swim fins for tropical currents and a wet suit for high-country glacial lakes might be the only way to get up close and personal with my subjects. While I was still in the bliss of embarking on a new adventure, what had Linda wondering if we could keep our heads above water on this project was not how many different dogs we needed to photograph in a finite time frame but the minor detail of how to photograph them on surfboards, kayaks, SUPs (stand-up paddleboards), canoes, and anything else nonmotorized that would float.

I started spending time at beaches, lagoons, rivers, and lakes, hoping to spot dogs and their owners out for a paddle. As optimistic as I am, my first reality check came when I saw dogs bounding along the riverbanks, splashing on the shorelines,

OH BOY, DID SOMEONE SAY
WE'RE GOING PADDLIN'?

and hurling themselves into the surf. There was no shortage of dogs in the water, but very few were on paddling devices. I made a point to never leave home without my own paddling devices. Dog owners were eager to sign up their dog, but if Bowser wasn't already a paddlin' dog, he wasn't always enthusiastic about hopping in or on one of these watersport contraptions, even for just a click of the camera. It was time for me to teach Doggie Paddling 101 to get the reluctant pooches comfortable if not excited about the joys of paddling or simply floating. Treats, balls, squeaky toys, reassuring rubs, an enthusiastic tone, focus, and patience and we had a crash-course formula that worked.

My first subject was our senior rescue dog, the gentle little Gypsy. We slipped on his yellow raincoat, helped him into a float tube, and let him paddle back and forth in front of a seasonal waterfall off one of his favorite hiking trails. Once all our friends' dogs were enlisted for paddling classes and photos, I had to venture out for more models.

I began actively recruiting, approaching every dog owner I encountered. "Does your dog like water?" "Oh, no, he won't go near it" was a common response. "Yes, she loves the water" was music to my ears. I gave my pitch and scheduled a time and location for the photo shoot. Although we live within walking distance of a river and barely a drive to an estuary and Pacific beaches, Mother Nature loves the suspense of her seasonal rhythms on the California coast. How long will the river flow this year? Will the river breach the sand and dry out the lagoon? Will the surf be gentle, or will there be "flip the dog off the surfboard" conditions? Mother Nature kept my photographing window limited.

The sunny, warm, dry summers at Mammoth Lakes in the Eastern Sierra, even with the occasional wicked winds and monsoon showers, were the perfect gift for the project. The bounty of lakes, many with marinas for kayaks, SUPs, paddle-boats, and canoe rentals, was a boon. Sadly, Gypsy had gone over Rainbow Bridge a few months earlier, as all our beloved furry family members eventually do; but Gem, a sweet young Siberian husky that had joined our pack, was always up for any adventure. She was so comfortable on and in water, we called her our Siberian water dog. One paddle on the lake with Linda, and she never hesitated to hop in the kayak or on a SUP. She eagerly lapped up the adulation from other paddlers and boaters, who were amazed to see a husky on a board, let alone one looking so poised as I clicked her photogenic poses.

By the time the season was in full swing in the Sierra, lakes, campgrounds, and hiking trails were buzzing with four-legged vacationers, and I had a potential new crop of models. I made several daily appointments to meet my recruits at the lake. Rather than taking a chance for the enthusiasm to cool off with "volunteer's remorse," at times we immediately walked to the closest marina for the shoot. Just because a dog likes being in the water doesn't mean he likes being *on* the water. Nor does a dog owner's being on board mean his or her dog would get *on* the board. But never underestimate the power of the treat for bribing and the squeak

I DON'T LOOK SO SHORT NOW, DO I?

MAYBE WE
SHOULD
PADDLE
DOWNWIND.

of a toy hidden in your shirt for focus. I would have carried a roasted chicken or a slab of ribs in my pack if that is what it took to convince dogs they wanted to be paddling stars. As it turned out, most of them were happy to extort a handful of liver treats in exchange for venturing out of their comfort zone. Dog owners walked away beaming with pride that Fido was starting to think of paddling as pretty cool stuff with unexpected rewards. For many dog owners the experience planted the seed for a whole new chapter of potential activities and fun adventures with Rover.

As the summer progressed, more dogs popped up out on the water, many keen paddlin' dogs.

Soon aspens began to flicker from green to gold, crowds thinned on the mountain lakes, and the pool of models was down to shallow. Having heard about surfing contests in Southern California, we migrated to new paddling territory and took the photo safari up a notch to Huntington Beach for the Surf City Surf Dog Competition.

The SUP workshop and the surf contest screamed "photo bonanza!" As if riding ocean waves isn't athletically challenging enough for dogs, come surf day the fall sky was blue with hot beach weather, but the waves were bigger and choppier than for any previous contest year. Gem was entered, but the conditions were just too rough for her surfing debut, so we scratched her. The show went off mostly as scheduled, and what a show it was, with dogs flying into the air, diving off their boards, being tossed around like beach balls or swamped by crashing waves. My camera never stopped clicking. Dogs had flotation vests, and each team (dog and owner) wore colored T-shirts to identify them in the heat categories. Each dog was assigned a junior lifeguard to maximize safety. From "Let's get this over with" to "Bring it on," every dog's body language sent a clear message.

A few weeks later, it was aloha time for our paddlin' dog photo shoot finale. We dropped our bags at the hotel and walked up Waikiki Beach. I asked a group of surfers if they knew of anyone who surfed with his or her dog. They had two words for me: "Duke's OceanFest," part of the birthday celebration for famous surfer Duke Kahanamoku. Unfortunately the event had been held a month earlier.

I was deflated but not defeated. After some sleuthing, I followed the thread to the event organizers and some of the contestants still on the island. My determination was rewarded with several responses, including from Alika Vaquer and his Jack Russell terrier Luna, best tandem ride winners of the 2016 Duke's OceanFest.

We flew home with a dozen more photographs of adorable paddling dogs. My favorite was a sunset shot of a family and their dog in an outrigger canoe.

I was thrilled to wrap up the assignment with plenty of photographs of paddling dogs, but the lasting memory is having the opportunity to meet dogs of all ages and pedigrees, from sweet mutts to regal rare breeds, all with great owners

Whether the *Doggie Paddlin'* photographs inspire you to take to the water with your four-legged companion or provide you with the vicarious enjoyment of seeing others paddling with their dogs, we hope this happy and fun book about truly our best friends enriches your days with smiles.

Meet the
PADDLIN' DOGS

WHAT?
YOU'VE NEVER SEEN A PRINCESS ON A KAYAK?

OKAY, I'VE GOT THIS BALANCE THING DOWN; LET'S HIT THE WATER.

YOU SURE YOU HAVE ENOUGH TREATS
FOR THIS VOYAGE?

I HOPE THAT KID DOESN'T MISS HIS TUBE.

YOU PROMISE THERE ARE SOME NEW SMELLS
OUT ON THE LAKE?

HEY, COME ON; IT'S MY TURN TO USE THE FLOTATION VEST.

DOES THIS BOARD MAKE ME LOOK FAT?

YOU BET I MAKE SURE HE BLOWS IT UP ALL THE WAY.

WELL, UP
HERE THE
WIND IS
COMING
FROM
THE LEFT.

HE'S ALWAYS HAPPIER WHEN I GO WITH HIM.

I THINK THE KAYAK'S COLOR MATCHES MY EYES.

HOW DO YOU LIKE THIS POSE?

YOU *ARE* GOING WITH ME, AREN'T YOU?

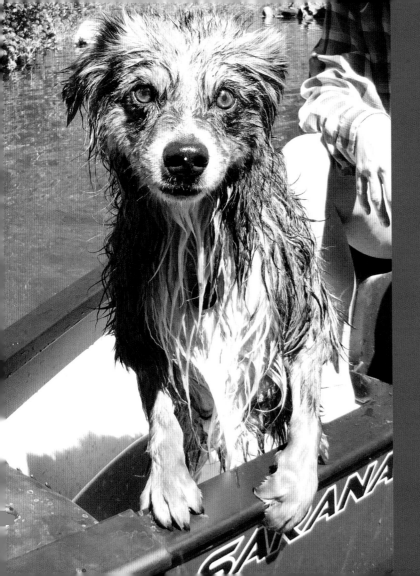

I WAS
HOPING TO
STAY DRY.

I WOULD RATHER KEEP MY EYES ON YOU.

I'VE GOT THIS ONE LOCKED!

I AM STRICTLY A TROPICAL SURFER.

SHE CAN'T GO ANYWHERE WITHOUT ME.

I TRY TO STAY AWAY
FROM THAT PADDLE.

DON'T
EXPECT
ME TO
GET ALL
EXCITED.

THE SHORE LOOKS A LOT FARTHER AWAY
THAN I REMEMBER.

WE KNOW WE'RE CUTE. CAN WE HAVE OUR TREAT NOW?

I AM DEFINITELY "IN THE ZONE."

AS LONG AS I GET TO RIDE IN FRONT, I'M GAME.

Dare Devil

I'M SURE GLAD I WORE MY RAINCOAT.

DOES THE HAT LOOK GOOD?
DOES THE HAT LOOK GOOD?

THAT BEACH UP THERE LOOKS LIKE A GOOD PLACE TO PLAY FRISBEE.

SHE SHOULD BE WORRIED ABOUT GETTING THOSE NEW SHOES WET.

OKAY, YOU'VE GOT OUR ATTENTION.

OKAY, THAT'S THE LAST PHOTO; LET'S GET PADDLIN'.

HE NEEDS THE LESSONS MORE THAN I DO.

THERE'S ROOM FOR A COUPLE OF MY BUDDIES.

I CHANGED MY MIND.

THAT'S MY
FAVORITE
SCARF FOR
KAYAKING.

DO I HAVE, LIKE, THE PERFECT FORM?

I CAN HYPNOTIZE OTHER DOGS WITH THE BLUE ONE.

PLUS RIDING DOESN'T FLOP YOUR EARS.

I'LL TAKE TWO 8 × 10S OF THIS POSE.

YOU REALLY THINK THOSE CLOUDS MATCH MY FUR?

THIS DEFINITELY DOES NOT FEEL RIGHT.

I LOVE THIS
CALM WATER.

ARE YOU SURE THE RACE
IS TODAY?

OOH, THAT WATER IS SALTY.

OF COURSE I'M UP FOR IT.
"WATER" IS MY MIDDLE NAME.

I FEEL LIKE I'M ON THE *TITANIC.*

THIS BOARD IS PLENTY BIG ENOUGH FOR ME.

CAN'T RIDE MUCH FARTHER THAN THIS.

I THINK I DESERVE A "10" FOR STYLE. WHAT DO YOU THINK?

I'M KNOWN FOR MY GRACEFUL DISMOUNTS.

WHAT,
YOU
DON'T
REALLY
THINK I
WOULD
JUMP?

HEY, FOUR ON THE FLOOR . . . I MEAN BOARD.

HOW LONG
BEFORE YOU
ARE READY?

I TALKED
HIM INTO
PADDLIN'
DOWN THE
RIVER.

ONLY ON HALLOWEEN!

HOW DID I GET UP HERE?

I'M THE GIRL; I GET THE RIBBON.

I FEEL LIKE I'M IN A WASHING MACHINE.

OKAY, I'LL
GO FOR A
SHORT RIDE.

I'M RIDIN' THE WILD SURF.

I GOT MY SUMMER TRIM JUST FOR PADDLIN'.

ABANDON SHIP!

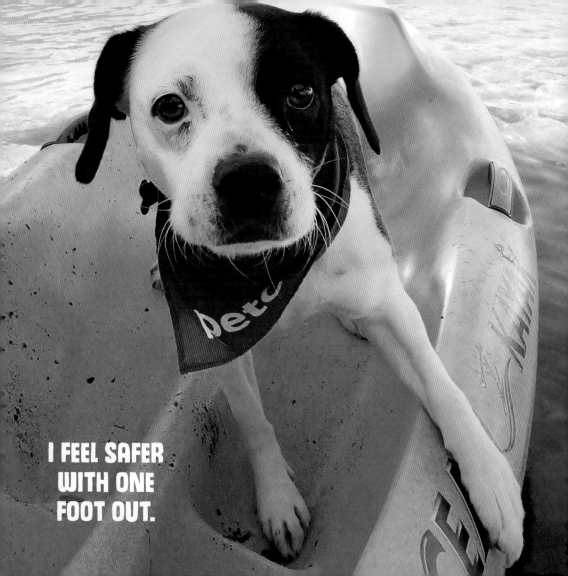

I FEEL SAFER
WITH ONE
FOOT OUT.

THERE'S A BIG ONE COMING ON THE OUTSIDE.

IT'S THE COLD WATER THAT MAKES
ME GRIT MY TEETH.

THAT WAS A WIPEOUT!

WE'RE READY TO HEAD HOME.

NO, I GET THE PADDED SEAT.

IF THE WIND CATCHES MY EARS,
WE WON'T NEED THE PADDLE.

IS IT ME THAT'S SMALL OR THE BOARD THAT'S BIG?

I AM REALLY GETTING AIR ON THIS RIDE.

I'M WORRIED ABOUT THE SUN WRINKLING MY SKIN TOO.

A LITTLE TO THE LEFT . . .

I THINK
HE
MISSED
THE
TURN
BACK
THERE.

I THINK I'M HEADED OVER THE FALLS.

COME ON, YOU PROMISED US A TREAT.

OKAY, GIVE ME A GOOD PUSH.

YOU SURE
YOU WANT
TO GO OUT
TODAY?

DON'T WORRY; I'M READY FOR THE BUMP.

REALLY, I DO
HAVE EARS
UNDER
THERE.

NOW *THIS* IS THE LIFE.

I'M THE ORIGINAL PADDLIN' DOG.

IT'S NOT AS SCARY FACING THIS WAY.

I THINK WE HAVE RUN AGROUND.

I DON'T HAVE A GOOD FEELING ABOUT THIS.

HEY, HE GOT THE
SAND ON THE
BOARD, NOT ME.

STOP PADDLIN';
I THINK I SEE A FISH!

IT'S A ONE-
OF-A-KIND
SURFING
HARNESS.
DO YOU
LIKE IT?

OKAY, I THINK WE'VE GOT THIS WAVE.

THAT WAS FUN. LET'S GO OUT AGAIN.

THAT COULD BE TROUBLE.

YOU PROMISE THIS IS GOING TO BE FUN?

I WOULDN'T HAVE WORN MY WINTER COAT IF I KNEW WE WERE COMING TO THE ISLANDS.

THAT WAS A GREAT DAY OF PADDLIN'.

THEY CALL ME
STEALTH DOG.

Becomin' a
PADDLIN' DOG

TRAINING YOUR DOG FOR PADDLIN'

IS YOUR DOG A PADDLIN' DOG ALREADY, or does he or she need to be taught to love paddling with you?

If you have a breed that naturally runs full speed into the water, like a Labrador or golden retriever or a Portuguese water dog, you have a head start on training your dog to be a paddling pal. But if you have a breed that is generally shy of water, like a Chihuahua, Rhodesian ridgeback, or Siberian husky, you probably have some hurdles to overcome.

In photographing paddling dogs for this book, we met puppies that bounced and frolicked in the water instinctively, dogs that were hesitant to approach a kayak, and dogs that refused to make contact with a drop of water. But we also watched the process of reluctant dogs becoming comfortable in the water and on a paddling device (PD) with their owner. We realized that with gentle patience and confident handling, along with sensitivity to the dog's reluctance and anxieties as well as understanding of its personality, even the most unlikely candidates could discover the joy of becoming a paddling companion.

If you start with a puppy (about twelve weeks old, after the first series of immunizations), bear in mind that everything in the world is new and can be

FRIENDS CAN MAKE PLAYING IN THE WATER MORE ENTICING.

SOME DOGS PREFER THE BEACH
RATHER THAN THE WATER.

intimidating, including water. Even a dog raised inland and comfortable around lakes and streams can be apprehensive at the ocean, with its breaking waves and water surging in and out.

If you've adopted what you thought was a "water dog" from a shelter and he or she appears to dislike or even fear water, that may be the result of a traumatic experience in its former life. You will need lots of patience to build trust and recondition your dog to enjoy water. You want to ease reluctant dogs into "water comfort" and have them associate water with positive, pleasurable activities, experiences, and rewards. Help them discover that there's joy to be had around water by looking, sniffing, and touching water at their own pace. As strange as it may seem, even breeds known to have an instinctual affinity for water (Labradors, golden retrievers, poodles, and Portuguese water dogs, to name a few popular breeds) may produce individuals that do not like water at all.

Following are twelve steps and basic do's and don'ts to forge the bond that will help your dog become a Paddlin' Dog.

1. DO take your dog near a small body of calm water like a pond. His reaction to the water will help you evaluate his comfort level around

water and his potential as a paddling companion. If you live near the ocean, pick a place and time when the tide is low and the water flat.

2. DON'T force your dog to go in the water by pulling her in at the end of a leash or tossing her in. The goal is to create a positive pleasurable association with water, not to bully your dog out of her comfort zone.

3. DO play with your dog near water. Sit in the water if necessary, and entice him to you with his favorite toy. Feed him tasty treats as close to the water as he will come and eventually with at least his paws in the water. Tell him what a good dog he is for being in the water.

4. DO consider using a child's wading pool in your backyard if you don't have access to a natural body of water, and then use the same technique as in step 3.

5. Most dogs love to play with other canine buddies. DO arrange for a playdate with a friend or neighbor's water-loving dog. Many dogs will brave new experiences if they are shown the way by another dog. Young dogs learn from older dogs.

GETTING YOUR DOG TO PLAY NEAR THE WATER IS AN IMPORTANT STEP.

REASSURE
AND MAKE
YOUR DOG
FEEL SAFE
IN THE
WATER.

6. Whether your dog is already comfortable in the water or still at the reticent or tentative stage, DO put your paddling device in the house or yard and let your dog get used to seeing and sniffing it for a few days. Be nonchalant about sitting on or in your device for a few minutes a day when your dog is around. Reward her with a treat when she comes nosing around you. Draw her on it with "high value" treats like bits of her favorite human food, and give her verbal praise and body rubs as a reward for the behavior you want to reinforce. Reward her with several small bites rather than just a single treat. For dogs it's the number of treat bites, not the size, that makes an impression. The longer she stays on the PD, the more treats she gets. It's also helpful to use a short leash and make walking across the PD (SUP or surfboard) part of an exercise so that the dog learns there's nothing unusual about the device. You're not alarmed by it, so why should she be? Having a treat at your side to encourage the dog as you walk across the PD may distract her from the fact that she is stepping on something "new" and build her confidence that the PD won't swallow her whole. Practice sitting on the PD on land with your dog and have her in the correct position for optimum balance. Typically the dog is in front of you in a sitting position. The more experienced the dog owner is on the PD and comfortable with balance, the easier it will be for both paddler and dog to share the device confidently.

Once your dog has learned to sit calmly on the PD on land, it will be easier to transfer that experience to being on the water. You want a nonslippery area on your PD so that your dog will have traction there. Consider adding a nonslip pad to your PD. Some people place a bath mat with suction cups at the location where their dog will sit or stand. Foam paddleboards and surfboards allow your pooch to grip the surface easier.

7. Once your dog is comfortable being with you on your PD, then simulate being on the water. Act as though you are paddling your PD. Tip and wiggle the device to simulate its movement on the water. At first your dog might be startled and jump off. Bring him back with treats and simulate again, gently so as not to scare or startle him.

8. DO practice your sit, down, and stay commands while your dog is getting on and getting off your PD. You want to be able to control her getting on and off your PD once you arrive at the water. If she jumps off unexpectedly, chances are you are going in the water too.

9. DO get your dog used to a flotation vest. Take him to the pet store to fit him with the correct size and style for his weight and physique.

INVITE YOUR DOG ONTO YOUR PADDLING DEVICE; DON'T FORCE HIM.

LET YOUR POOCH GET COMFORTABLE WITH YOU ON THE PADDLING DEVICE ON LAND BEFORE GOING ON THE WATER.

Make sure it has a strong handle on top so you can lift your dog. DO have him wear it around the house for short periods so that he gets used to having it put on and taken off and moving about wearing it. Combine putting the vest on him with giving him a treat. If your dog is not food motivated, you can combine putting the vest on with playing one of his favorite games (throwing the ball or tug-of-war with a chew toy). Reinforce the desired behavior by connecting it to whatever your dog considers a reward. Have him wear the vest when he gets on your paddling device. Have him wear it in the water before he gets on the PD. He needs to learn what it can do for him—help him float and make maneuvering in the water easier.

10. DO take your PD to the lake, river, or ocean you plan to float on. Put the paddling device on the shore and repeat the on-and-off, in-and-out routines you've practiced at home. Your dog should be wearing her flotation vest and be on a short leash. DO use rewards and verbal praise to continue building your dog's confidence around the PD. DON'T rush the process by taking to the water too soon with your dog on the PD. Encourage your dog to sit on the PD in the area you want her when you are on the water.

11. Once Pooch is comfortable around, on, and in your paddling device, slide it to the water's edge and then gently slide part of it into the water. Give your dog lots of verbal reassurance. If he jumps off, back up a step, lure him back with a treat, and continue. He should be wearing his flotation vest and a leash attached to his collar. DON'T attach the leash to the PD. It's safer to hold the leash as a way to stay connected to your dog if he jumps or falls off the PD. That way you can always let go of the leash if necessary. Attaching the leash to the PD increases the risk of your dog getting tangled or strangled by the leash. Some flotation vests have rings on the back to attach the leash rather than to the collar.

12. Once you feel confident that your dog is reasonably comfortable on the PD, it's time to go farther out into the water. You may want to keep a leash attached to your dog's flotation vest, but not attached to your PD, to help you retrieve her if you become separated. It there is a chance the leash might get tangled on your PD or on anything in the water, don't use a leash. Don't be discouraged if your dog seems nervous or has second thoughts about this new adventure. It helps to have a friend assist with the first launch so that you can hold and reassure your dog. Many dogs that exhibit anxiety at leaving shore relax very quickly once they are afloat. Enjoy

INITIALLY, JUST SITTING WITH YOUR POOCH CAN BUILD BOTH YOUR CONFIDENCE.

START WITH SMALL WAVES WHEN TEACHING YOUR DOG TO SURF.

your first of many paddles with your paddling pal. Keep the first few outings short (ten to fifteen minutes) and close to shore. Build on the successes to share safe quality bonding time on water with your dog. If it turns out your dog thinks it was too soon for the test launch, he just needs more time to boost his confidence and trust. Just slow down and repeat steps 1–12.

FLOTATION VESTS HELP YOUR DOG BE MORE BUOYANT.

APPENDIX A: PADDLIN' CHECKLIST

- ☐ Paddling device
- ☐ Paddle
- ☐ Personal flotation jacket
- ☐ Dog flotation vest
- ☐ Leash
- ☐ Dog treats
- ☐ Fresh water for drinking and rinsing
- ☐ Sunblock
- ☐ Hat
- ☐ Sunglasses
- ☐ First-aid kit
- ☐ Towels
- ☐ Waterproof camera

APPENDIX B: RESOURCES

Airheadsup.com	Dog paw pads for SUP
Bettersurfthansorry.com	No-skid pads for SUP
Chewy.com	Flotation vests
Hotdogcollars.com	Reflective waterproof dog collars
Petmountain.com	Flotation vests
Ruffwear.com	Flotation vests and other gear
Sitstay.com	Waterproof collars

APPENDIX C: DOG SURFING EVENTS

Duke's OceanFest, August
Going to the Dogs SurFur Competition
Honolulu, Hawaii
dukesoceanfest.com

Hang 20 Surf Dog Classic, August
Kite Beach, Jupiter, Florida
(561) 747-5311
furryfriendsadoption.org

Noosa Festival of Surfing, March
noosafestivalofsurfing.com
Vetshop Australia Dog Surfing
    Challenge
Shire of Noosa, Queensland, Australia

Ohana Surf Dog Competition, July
Galveston Island Humane Society
Galveston Island, Texas
galvestonhumane.org
(409) 740-1919

Surf Dog Surf-A-Thon Surf Dog
    Competition, September
Helen Woodward Animal Center
Del Mar Dog Beach, Del Mar,
    California
animalcenter.org
(858) 756-4117

Unleashed by Petco Surf City Surf
    Dog Competition, September
Huntington Beach, California
surfdogevents.com

Unleashed by Petco Surf Dog
    Competition, July–August
Imperial Beach, California
surfdogevents.com

World Dog Surfing Championship, August
Linda Mar Beach, Pacifica, California
surfdogchampionships.com

APPENDIX D: THE PADDLIN' DOGS

NAME/AGE(if available)/BREED

Amadei/9/Blue merle collie
Ashby/1/Scottish terrier
Aspen/2/Mix
Autumn/3/Redbone coonhound
Bada/9/Jindo
Bailey/4/Rhodesian ridgeback
Bamboo/?/Double doodle
Beans/4/Whippet
Bella/7/Tibetan spaniel–longhair dachs-
   hund
Bentley/1/Golden Lab
Bentley/2/Maltese
Bixby/1/Bailey/2/Standard poodles
Bodhi/6/Black dachshund
Bodie/9/Brittany spaniel
Bonnie/?/Border collie
Bono/?/Labrador retriever
Bosley/2/French bulldog
Brandy the Pug/7/Pug
Brody/?/Labradoodle

Brooklyn/?/Labrador retriever
Bugz/?/Chihuahua
Buster/4/Boxer
Caesar/3/ German shepherd
Cherie/5/French bulldog
Chico Chip/2/Micro & Coco Puff/2/
   Miniature Chihuahua
Chryssy/7/German shepherd mix
Cody/8 months/Pit bull–Labrador re-
   triever
Cookie/10/Miniature dachshund
Deliah/?/Cavalier King Charles spaniel
Delilah/4 months/Golden retriever
Derby/?/Goldendoodle
Dickens/2/Portuguese water dog
Dory/10/Wirehair dachshund
Emmy/5/Golden retriever
Finn/?/Golden retriever/Scouter/?/
   Terrier mix
Finnegan/3/ Cockapoo
Gem/2/Siberian husky
Guinness/5/Black Lab

Gypsy/10/Chihuahua mix
Han Solo/1/Mix
Haole/8/Yellow Lab
Hina/6/Labrador retriever
Honzo/7/Boxer
Ikaika/4/ American pit bull terrier
Jackie/12/Jack Russell terrier
Jake/7/Border collie McNab
Joey/11/Terrier
Joey/2/Miniature pinscher
Kalani/8/Red golden retriever
KeaWai/4/Labradoodle
Koa/2/American pit bull terrier
Koda/4 months/Husky
Kona Kai/?/Labradoodle
Kui/?/?
Lani/?/Labradoodle
Lexa/1/Golden retriever
Libby/7/Queensland heeler
Loki/12/Silky terrier/Puck/11/Shih tzu
Lola/9/Beagle–German shepherd
Luke/8/German shepherd
Luna/11/Jack Russell terrier
Maggie/?/Tobey/?/Pugs
Major/2/Mix

Maple/4/Terrier mix
Marcello/10/Spinone Italiano
Maxamillion/6 months/American
    Eskimo dog
Maxi/10/Shih tzu mix
Maya/6 months/Maltese–Yorkshire ter-
    rier
Mickey/4 months/Goldendoodle
Misty/3 months/Herby/3/Sunny/3/
    Boston terriers
Mocha/1/Labradoodle
Monster/6/Briard
Nala/1/German shepherd
Nala/4/Shepherd-Malamute
Nala/?/Chocolate Lab/Bear/?/Golden
    retriever
Nigel/4/Labradoodle
Odie/1/Springer spaniel
Olive/7/Emma/1/Chesapeake Bay
    retrievers
Oso/8/Labrador–Great Dane
Otis/1/Yellow Lab
Parafina/?/Mix
Peanut/4/Cavachon
Pele/4/Labrador–French mastiff

Penny/8/Shepherd mix
Perrita/4/Chihuahua-dachshund/
    Nelson/4/Puggle
Phia/4/Doberman pinscher/
    Journey/10/Rat terrier
Phoebe/3/Shih tzu
Piper/4/Silky terrier
Prince Dudeman/8/Bichon frise–
    Japanese chin
Puggie/13/Pug
Quinn/4/Bernese mountain dog
Rascal/13/Mix
Raven/13/Labrador retriever
Rawley/6/Rottweiler
Red/3/Black mouth cur
Reina/7/German shepherd mix
Rex/?/Cockapoo
Rico/?/American pit bull terrier
Riley/8/Maltipoo
Ritter/2/Labradoodle
Rover/4/Setter–Staffordshire bull terrier
Roxie/4/Staffordshire terrier
Ryder Splash/2/Moyen parti poodle
Sam/5/Labrador–sheepdog
Sassy/12/Dachshund

Sawyer/3/Rhodesian ridgeback
Skyler/5/Queensland heeler
Smith/2/Jack Russell terrier
Sparky/13/Bichon frise
Sugar/?/Collie mix
Sully/7/English bulldog
Taffy/10/Welsh Pembroke corgi
Tahoe/8/Golden Lab mix
Tai/3/Black Lab–greyhound
Teddy/15/Pomeranian
Teddy/2/Goldendoodle
Teddy/5/Shih tzu
Thor/9/Old English bulldog
Tia/?/Papillion
Tobey/4/Chihuahua
Tristan/4/West Highland white terrier
Tucker/3/Goldendoodle
Verona/5/Spinone Italiano
Walter/7/Dachshund
Whiskey/1/Terrier mix
Yolo/4/Mini Australian shepherd
Zachary/3/Poodle

ACKNOWLEDGMENTS

This book would not have been possible without all the wonderful dogs and their owners who were willing to have their photographs taken and shared with you.

We especially want to thank the following, who provided information, assistance, and use of their equipment for the photographs: Don and Joe at Lake Mary Marina, Mammoth Lakes, California; Tammy, Dylan, and Luciano at Pokonobe Marina, Mammoth Lakes, California; Roy, Matt, and Vicky at Tamarack Lodge, Mammoth Lakes, California; Pirate Coast Paddle Company, Newport Beach, California; Lisa, Jodi, and Marcie at Surf City Surf Dog, Huntington Beach, California; Kelli at Duke's OceanFest, Honolulu, Hawaii; Kono's Restaurants, Oahu, Hawaii; John at Go Bananas Watersports, Honolulu, Hawaii. Errol at Hawaii Hot Spots, Waikiki, Hawaii; Chris, Sup Dog Oz, Queensland, Australia.

ABOUT THE AUTHORS

DAVID AND LINDA MULLALLY have been a photographer/writer team for more than thirty years. They share a passion for dogs, travel, and the outdoors on land and water. They have been writing about dogs for more than twenty-five years, including David as the first travel photographer and Linda as travel columnist for *Dog Fancy* magazine. They have coauthored numerous hiking guides, several of

which focus on dog-friendly hiking trails. *Doggie Paddlin'* is their tenth book, with more works in progress. David, Linda, and Gem, their paddleboarding Siberian husky, make Carmel and Mammoth Lakes, California, their base camp.